D0066255

101 WAYS TO SPOIL
YOUR WIFE

by Ron Brown

HONOR **HB** BOOKS

Inspiration and Motivation for the Seasons of Life

COOK COMMUNICATIONS MINISTRIES
Colorado Springs, Colorado • Paris, Ontario
KINGSWAY COMMUNICATIONS LTD
Eastbourne, England

Honor Books® is an imprint of
Cook Communications Ministries, Colorado Springs, CO 80918
Cook Communications, Paris, Ontario
Kingsway Communications, Eastbourne, England

101 WAYS TO SPOIL YOUR WIFE
© 2000 by RON BROWN

Printed in Canada
Printing/Year
5 4 3 2 / 05 06

Unless otherwise indicated, all Scripture references are taken from the *King James Version* of the Bible. Scripture quotations marked NIV are taken from *The Holy Bible: New International Version*® NIV®. Copyright © 1973, 1978, 1984, by International Bible Society. Used by permission of Zondervan Publishing House. All rights reserved.

ISBN: 1-56292-814-7

INTRODUCTION

Woman! The thought of her excites me. Sometimes it's *WOW*man, and other times it's *WO*man! Everything about my wife still takes my breath away. She inspires me, ignites me, comforts me, and intrigues me. She is the reason I have written this simple "suggestion" book. If anyone in my life deserves to be spoiled, it is my wife.

This world offers all the things your heart desires—a bigger house, that new car, a big boat, golf clubs. We don't always calculate the "real cost" of going after what we want. Things may bring temporary happiness, but have we overlooked the real source of happiness? Our family. More marriages would be lasting if the wives were spoiled as they deserve.

It is long overdue for us men to step forward, be men, and start showing the women in our lives how vital they are to us. Most men don't want to show emotion or affection in public. We feel ashamed and wonder, *What if the other guy sees me?* To which I say, "Who cares?!" My wife is a precious gift to me, and I will forever give her whatever she needs. I am not embarrassed to be seen giving to my wife.

Wives raise our children, prepare our meals, wash our clothes, and clean the house—and all of this usually after a long hard day at work. They help us in ways difficult to measure. They support our decisions. They help us see what we often can't. They help us be real. I have never gotten over the excitement my wife brings to me. She makes my shirt buttons pop!

This simple book offers you suggestions for spoiling your wife. You may laugh at some of the ideas, but I can assure you, *she won't*. If you will make sure she knows how much you love her, you will create a long-lasting marriage and bond between you that cannot be broken. That, my friend, is refreshing!

The new house will need repair, the car will lose its shine, the boat will get old, golf may get dull. What will you have left? I want to go through my life knowing that I put my time and love into what gives back to me. I want to say, "I do" with my *life*.

Want a great marriage? Then this book is a must for you. Who can find a virtuous woman? I did. How about you?

—Ron Brown

1.

ONE

Make sure you tell her every day that she is
your best friend, your lover, and your confidant.
There should never be a doubt in her mind how
you feel about her. She needs you to tell her
and show her how important she is to you.

A friend loveth at all times.
Proverbs 17:17

2.
TWO

No matter how long you've been married, make sure you take her back to the place you first met and fell in love. It is important to her that her man makes this a priority. This will help keep those first magical moments dose to your heart. Women cherish this.

Let thy fountain be blessed: and rejoice with the wife of thy youth.
Proverbs 5:18

3.
THREE

Even if you cant sing, try it! Sing her some special, romantic song that you know she likes, maybe even get down on one knee and sing.

Put away your pride and just do it. It's one of those "being a fool for her" things that she will adore. I make a habit of singing to my wife. Tena. quite often. We have a list of favorite romantic songs that we both share. I usually sing to her in the car. with or without the radio or CD player. She loves to hear me sing (even though I'm not that great). But the memory will forever be special to her. She loves knowing I'm singing to her.

4.

FOUR

Save your money and take her shopping. Let her shop 'til she drops.

Hint: If you are in the "doghouse" for
something, this is a good way to get out.

*Love is patient, love is kind. It does not envy, it does not boast, it is
not proud. It is not rude. it is not self-seeking, it is not easily
angered. it keeps no record of wrongs. . . . Love never fails.*

1 Corinthians 13:4-8 NIV

I made the mistake of letting Tena go shopping with my mom
one day. Oh boy! Mom had all the fun watching Tena try on all
these clothes. In fact. Mom encouraged her to "buy them all."
(Thanks, Mom. I thought you were on my side.) My mother
bought nothing that day. Tena, however, came home with seven
new outfits. That one shopping trip hurt for a long time. Tip:
Mom can visit only once a year.

5.
FIVE

This one takes a real man to do. Turn off the ball
game on Sunday afternoon, and take her
to the local park for a picnic. (Go ahead, laugh
if you want to, but this will mean more to your
relationship than any ball game ever will.)

Endeavoring to keep the unity of the Spirit in the bond of peace.
Ephesians 4:3

10

6.
SIX

Sometime, somehow, somewhere, marry her all over again. You could keep it simple, or go all out and invite lots of friends, family, etc.— celebrate your love all over again.

Live joyfully with the wife whom thou lovest all the days of the life of thy vanity. which he hath given thee under the sun.
Ecclesiastes 9:9

7.

Handle the finances. Pay the bills, mail them, make the deposits, and set a budget. Just take care of things, so she doesn't have to. It's called "being a leader:"

He that handleth a matter wisely shall find good.
Proverbs 16:20

Okay, I admit it. I'm the perfectionist in the family. One time we decided Tena would handle the paying of the bills. It lasted about a month. Oh, it's not that she couldn't stay on track, write the checks, and stay the course with our budget. It's that she stuck the stamped envelopes in her organizer and never mailed them. I don't think her organizer was working properly.

8.
EIGHT

Come home early from work one day and
prepare dinner. Totally surprise her and have
a meal prepared, table set, candles lit, and
dinner ready to serve when she comes in.

Now I know this is a BIG stretch for most men, but it will
score very well with the women. Check her cookbooks for ideas. or
if you just can't figure it out, call your mother. I'm telling you. she
simply won't believe it. But she will *love* it.

9.

NINE

Get together a group of friends and relatives and throw her a huge, surprise birthday party. Be creative. Pick a place and time, get the cake and decorations, and make it happen. I've done this, and she was shocked. It's not that hard. A few of her friends will be glad to help.

> Hint: Be sure you have the right calendar date.
> If you're going to remember her birthday
> in a big way, remember the right day.

I threw Tena a surprise party last year for her birthday. Two months earlier, I contacted her closest friends and family. She thought we were going to a company social that I had to attend. I even got her to bring three dozen of her own best cookies. Boy, you should have seen the shock in her eyes when we arrived. She is still talking about this one. This created a great memory for her that will last for years to come.

10.
TEN

Check into a hotel some weekend and give her a change of environment. If you can afford it, find a hotel with a massage therapist, steam room, nail salon, etc. (The longer she is out getting pampered, the longer you can check out the sports scene on TV.) Every woman loves to just get away from the same old routine every now and then, and this will be just what she needed.

Let the husband render unto the wife due benevolence.
1 Corinthians 7:3

11.
ELEVEN

Keep her car full of gas and clean at all times. (This is one of those things you should make a habit of doing all the time.) It's a "man" thing that she should never have to do.

Keeping your wife's car full of gas helps her—and you. I don't want my wife out at night filling a car with gas, or smelling like it, so I do it. Besides, one day in her haste, she drove off with the hose still in the tank, which ripped it from the pump. The local station wasn't too happy. I fill the gas tanks—she just turns the key and takes off.

12.
TWELVE

Okay, now take a deep breath: Invite her mom to come visit for the weekend. I know, I know, I've lost my mind. But, this has its advantages too! I usually get some pretty good meals while my mother-in-law is in town. You can always suggest that the two of them should go do something together, like shopping. Bingo, you score again.

I can do all things through Christ which strengtheneth me.
Philippians 4:13

13.
THIRTEEN

Send your wife romantic, thoughtful cards in the mail occasionally. You should always be a step ahead in thinking of these kinds of things. Keep your romance alive as much as possible.

Whoso findeth a wife findeth a good thing.
and obtaineth favour of the Lord.
Proverbs 18:22

This is another one of those things men tend to overlook. Just because we're men doesn't mean we can't be thoughtful. It should become a mindset that we adore our wives and let them know it.

14.
FOURTEEN

Take the trash out regularly! This is another
thing a wife should never have to do,
nor should she have to ask you to.

15.
FIFTEEN

Call her at home or work, and ask her out. It doesn't
matter how long you've been married; you can
still date! You can both have fun flirting by phone.
Tell her how attracted you are to her.

16.
SIXTEEN

Clean the entire house for her some day. (You will
need to know what all those cleaning products are
for before you start. For example, Mop'n' Glo is
not to shine your mop, nor is it for countertops.
Do not use Ajax on linoleum floors.) You will
have a whole new appreciation for what she does
at home. And for some women, all that housework
comes after a hard day's work at the office.

Carry each others burdens. and in this
way you will fulfill the law of Christ.
Galatians 6:2 NIV

17.
SEVENTEEN

Let her have quiet time to recharge her batteries.
If you have kids, get lost with them for a while.
Believe me, the whole family will benefit.

18.
EIGHTEEN

Surprise your wife with something that she loves: a bottle
of her favorite perfume, bath or shower gel, candy, or shoes.
(Hey, you can never go wrong with shoes!) Make sure you
know her size, or get her a gift certificate. Trust me.
This would be good for you newlyweds to learn.

It is more blessed to give than to receive.
Acts 20:35

19.
NINETEEN

Make a list and do the grocery shopping for her.
I find that the best time to go is early on Saturday
morning. When she awakens, let her know that
it is already done. Now, this is a big one, men.
(I hate shopping for groceries as much as you,
but remember, the goal here is to spoil her. I
never said it wouldn't take effort.)

Let us not love in word. neither in tongue; but in deed and in truth.
1 John 3:18

Come on, how hard can this be? You probably had to do the
shopping when you were single, so do it now. Who says it's a
woman's job? At least go with her and help out if you just can't go
alone. It's groceries, not quilting.

20.
TWENTY

When the kids are spending the night
somewhere else, rent her favorite movie and
watch it with her. (Sometimes this is torture
to me, but I try as often as I can. I'm trying to
get her interested in James Bond or action movies,
but it doesn't quite create the same mood.)

This one is tough for me, but the movies she likes usually
surprise me with a great truth or message. The older movies are
best if you really want one with a great story line. Look for old
Jimmy Stewart movies or her favorite actor or actress. Find out her
favorites and get them in advance.

21.
TWENTY-ONE

Always treat her with respect. Whether publicly or in private, your wife should be treated with more respect than anyone. She deserves it, and it is your obligation as a man. By all means, hold doors open for her, carry things, lift things, and help her if you have small children. Treat her like a queen.

Husbands. love your wives. even as Christ
also loved the church. and gave himself for it.
Ephesians 5:25

22.

When she comes home exhausted from
the day's work, have a big bubble bath waiting.

Hint: You might coordinate this the same night
you cook her that dinner. Who knows? There
might be a little something in it for you.

Blessed are the merciful: for they shall obtain mercy.
Matthew 5:7

This is easy. If you have any sense at all, you'll figure this one
out. You get home, light a few candles, rum on the soft music, run
her a hot bubble bath, and maybe have a flower in a vase by the tub.
You never know, she may get a second wind in no time at all.

23.
TWENTY-THREE

Do the laundry for her one day. I mean one day
because that's probably the last day she will let you
do it. (Read carefully! Whites with whites in hot
water, colors in cold water, and don't wash the silk
stuff! How do they remember all of these rules?)

Blessed are the pure in heart: for they shall see God.
Matthew 5:8

24.
TWENTY-FOUR

Be a constant encourager to your wife. If she is
financially helping the family by working, take time
to listen to her concerns or problems and offer your
help and support. Thank her for her contribution
regularly, and let her know you couldn't make it
without her. Gratitude goes such a long way.

A word fitly spoken is like apples of gold in pictures of silver.
Proverbs 25:11

25.
TWENTY-FIVE

Make sure you give her lots of affection. Hug her
often, kiss her, or come up behind her and wrap
your arms around her and just say, "I love you!"
If you are affectionate, she should never
have to wonder if you love her.

He that loveth not knoweth not God; for God is love.
1 John 4:8

26.

Pray for her every day, and let her know that you do. You don't know how to pray? Just begin by being thankful and the words will come. We should constantly lift up our wives in prayer.

The effectual fervent prayer of a righteous man availeth much.
James 5:16

I have whispered prayers of thankfulness for my wife many times. But. when I knew she was about to engage in "battle"—in a time of need or in a crucial meeting—I especially made an extra effort to pray. It is so miraculous to see God answer and work everything out. This will strengthen you as much as her. Prayer is a powerful weapon when your heart is right.

27.
TWENTY-SEVEN

Keep the temperature in the house and in the car
to her liking. (For some reason my wife is always
cold. Is yours?) We should find a happy medium
and make sure she is comfortable.

Husbands, love your wives, and be not bitter against them.
Colossians 3:19

28.
TWENTY-EIGHT

If she has a list of errands to run, do them
for her, or go with her to help out. Her time
is just as limited as yours, so why not take
the opportunity to just be together.

Sometimes, Tena and I spend half of the day on Saturday
running errands. If I didn't go with her, I would never see her. We
usually come back feeling like we accomplished a lot, and we had
the benefit of enjoying one another's company. We hit the cleaners,
the grocery store, the home improvement center, and the bookstore!
We love to be together.

29.

TWENTY-NINE

Pick up after yourself. She is *not* the maid!

By all means, guys. pick up. Help clean up. Your wife is not your maid. nor should she be. Don't expect your wife to do the simple things that you should do out of common courtesy and respect.

30.

THIRTY

Hire a maid every now and then to clean the entire house. This allows you and your wife time for more important matters.

"It will be good for that servant whom the master finds doing so when he returns."
Luke 12:43 NIV

31.

THIRTY-ONE

If she likes a lovely yard, create one and keep it that way. It's really that simple. Beautify her surroundings, so she can come home to her own paradise.

The steps of a good man are ordered by
the Lord: and he delighteth in his way.
Psalm 37:23

Being a landscape professional, I keep my yard picture pe[rfect] anyway. But you might not have thought about it. Even o[n a] budget, you can beautify your lawn. Fertilize regularl[y,] shrubs properly, plant spring and fall flowers that s[how,] keep the beds mulched. These are simple tasks tha[t] Your local home improvement center will ca[rry] serious landscapes if you desire. Check it out!

32.
THIRTY-TWO

Have flowers sent to her place of employment
or at home—maybe even at a social event or
a place where she volunteers. Whether it's for
a birthday, anniversary, or just to say, "I love you,"
every woman loves fresh flowers. (This will raise
your stock in the eyes of her co-workers too.)

Many waters cannot quench love. neither can the floods drown it.
Song of Solomon 8:7

33.
THIRTY-THREE

Never be selfish—not with your time, your energy,

or your things. What's yours is hers—all the time.

(If you don't believe it, just ask her.)

Give in and accept the fact that she will wear your clothes. When I can't find a shirt, I have a pretty good idea where it is. I just wish she wouldn't take my last bite of dessert. Do all women do this? Just accept the fact that she feels close enough to you to do these things.

34.
THIRTY-FOUR

Anytime your wife receives special recognition—
at the office, at church, in a dub, or in the
community-celebrate with her. If your wife
works outside of your home and gets a raise
or a promotion, make it a special occasion
and brag about how outstanding you think she is.
This way, you give her a raise too.

Let not mercy and truth forsake thee: bind them about
thy neck; write them upon the table of thine heart.
Proverbs 3:3

35.
THIRTY-FIVE

Give her a call when you hear her favorite song on the radio and share it with her. (Just put the phone to the radio when she answers. This is guaranteed to get a smile on the other end of the line.)

This does more than just bring back a romantic thought. Sometimes we both have tough. long days with plenty of demands and responsibilities. Taking time out to give her a call in the midst of chaos is just what we both need. It helps me get through a day when I know I can just get a tender voice on the other end of the line. This is why it is so important to be in love with your spouse.

36.
THIRTY-SIX

When she is extremely tired, let her go to bed early and sleep late. Put a "do not disturb" sign on her door and let her rest. You handle whatever needs handling and leave her alone.

37.
THIRTY-SEVEN

Write her a poem or romantic love note from your heart and then read it to her at just the right time. (You'll know when it's "just the right time.")

Pleasant words are as an honeycomb.
sweet to the soul. and health to the bones.
Proverbs 16:24

38.
THIRTY-EIGHT

If you play golf and she doesn't, take time
to teach her. Let her go with you sometime,
and you can both get frustrated together.

39.
THIRTY-NINE

Keep a few of your favorite pictures of
her in your wallet. Place them where you
can see her face every time you open it.

40.
FORTY

It's a universal rule: women love diamonds.
You can buy her one, or you can be one.

*Bow down thine ear, and hear the words of the wise,
and apply thine heart unto my knowledge.*
Proverbs 22:17

Diamonds. There's just something magical about them—the way they shine, the way they look, the way they make her feel. If you want to buy her one, she won't stop you. If you can't afford to give her a diamond, be one. Learn to shine, to sparkle, and to make her feel beautiful. Surround her with the best of you, and it will bring out the best in her.

41.
FORTY-ONE

Load the dishwasher yourself after dinner. Do this often.
If she prepared the meal, let her sit and rest while you
clean the kitchen. This will definitely be appreciated,
and it certainly won't hurt you to help out.

Hint: Use only recommended soap. One time I
loaded the dishwasher, but we were out of detergent.
I thought liquid dish soap would do the same thing,
so I put some in. I came back in the room fifteen
minutes later to find soap suds oozing out from
every conceivable crack. It took me longer to clean
up the floor than to wash the dishes one by one.

42.
FORTY-TWO

Listen to your wife. Really listen! Sometimes
she just needs to speak, and you just need to listen.
Part of being married is hearing intently what
the other has to say. (Trust me, guys; it
will save you a lot of heartache down
the road if you will heed this advice.)

He that hath ears to hear, let him hear.
Matthew 11:15

43.
FORTY-THREE

Give her a massage when she really needs it.

Just pamper her and rub out all

those aches and pains.

Admit it: You can't keep your hands off of her anyway, so why not "volunteer" to give her a massage? What the heck! She gets what she wants, and you get what you want. Then, later on, you may both get something you want.

44.

Don't fuss about the things she collects.
If it is important to her, then just live with it.
Life is too short for disharmony.

Withhold not good from them to whom it is due,
when it is in the power of thine hand to do it.
Proverbs 3:27

Collecting is one thing. but you also have to find a place to put the things she collects. Has your wife ever told you she needed a bigger house? Tena collects picture frames, silver boxes, dogs, people, books, birdhouses, and antiques. I think it's time to move to a warehouse or hold a huge garage sale!

45.
FORTY-FIVE

Tell her *often* how crazy you are about her, how good she looks, and how much you are attracted to her.

He that loveth his wife loveth himself.
Ephesians 5:28

46.
FORTY-SIX

Never go to bed at night with unresolved conflict between you. I promise it will not get better overnight, and you certainly won't get any sleep. Get it resolved!

Let not the sun go down upon your wrath.
Ephesians 4:26

47.

FORTY-SEVEN

Brag about her cooking. Whether it's breakfast, lunch, dinner, cookies, pies, or cakes: *brag, brag, brag!* Sooner or later, it's going to show up around your waistline anyway, so you might as well enjoy getting there.

48.

FORTY-EIGHT

Never be jealous of her. Let her have the time she needs away with friends, so she can share herself with others too. This will usually make her feel good about herself, and she will come back refreshed.

49.
FORTY-NINE

Make sure you do those gentle, romantic things
she loves. Light candles around the house, dance
with her, play music, or do whatever your wife loves.
Keep romance alive in everything you do.

May the Lord make your love increase and
overflow for each other and for everyone else.
1 Thessalonians 3:12 NIV

This is one of those things a lot of men think is not important
or is for sissies. Yet it's one thing that all women love. They need
those romantic things: music, dinner, or dancing. Keep it fresh and
exciting! I think it is important to keep "romancing" her long after
the vows have been taken.

50.
FIFTY

Take her out some lazy day for her favorite
ice cream cone. These simple gestures, men,
are things that are remembered in time.

As we have opportunity. let us do good to all people.
Galatians 6:10 NIV

Now. I realize this is no big deal to most of us. But it's one of
those simple things that is enjoyable any time of year. We usually
stop off at the local ice cream shop to get a cone. and then we go sit
down like kids and talk betWeen licks. When you can learn to do
simple things in life. it takes stress away and reminds you that life
doesn't have to be so complicated.

51.
FIFTY-ONE

Leave notes around the house where you know she will be. Write her notes of love or just notes to say "thank you" for being everything you need in a wife. Let her know you are thankful for her.

Now, this is really kind of fun to do. You may think it's corny, but my wife loves it! We don't go overboard, but when I write her simple love messages, they mean the world to her. She usually saves everything I write to her. There is still a note in our kitchen window that I wrote a few months ago. Why not make her feel special or brighten her day with a surprise love note?

52.
FIFTY-TWO

Skip work one afternoon, and run off somewhere
together. Maybe go to a movie or to her
favorite antique store. I'm sure you'll know just
what to do when you whisk her away.

Heaviness in the heart of man maketh it stoop:
but a good word maketh it glad.
Proverbs 12:25

53.
FIFTY-THREE

Shine your wife's shoes for her. Do this regularly.

Hint: This could save you a lot of money. Formerly
scuffed shoes that get a bright new shine could be
mistaken for actual new shoes. Who knows? Your wife
might discover those black shoes are actually blue.

The fact that you would take time to clean her shoes and
shine them will mean a lot to her. It's a simple service of love you
can provide to your wife that will keep her wondering how she ever
got so lucky.

54.

FIFTY-FOUR

Always give 100 percent of yourself to her.

Don't complain, and don't halfway do something.

Be committed; be outstanding.

Depart from evil, and do good; seek peace, and pursue it.
Psalm 34:14

55.
FIFTY-FIVE

Do anything you can to support
everything she does.

If your wife gets involved in a cause of any kind, stand beside her and help her. If she takes on a mission, get involved in whatever way she needs you to. Whether she volunteers for something or is just working late, do your part to help out and be the rock she can stand on. If she believes in her cause, then, by all means, so should you.

56.
FIFTY-SIX

See to it that your wife has plenty of pantyhose.
How many times has she put on the only pair
she can find, and they are full of runners?

Hint: Keep lots of nail polish on hand for quick repairs.

57.
FIFTY-SEVEN

If you have a baby in the family, *you* get up
at night to soothe the little one. There is
no written rule that says this is *her* job.

58.
FIFTY-EIGHT

Have a great attitude. Period. Since 90 percent
of life is our attitude, make sure yours
is healthy. Be a leader in this area to her,
as well as to the rest of your family.

Casting all your care upon him; for he careth for you.
1 Peter 5:7

I have to admit I am not always the best when it comes to
attitude. But when I sit back and realize that my attitude affects
the whole family, it really gets my attention. We should have the
best attitudes in our family if we are to be the leaders we should be.
Practice having a winning attitude. She will only want to be around
you more.

59.
FIFTY-NINE

Include your wife in all the things you can.
Let her be a part of whatever you do.

Only by pride cometh contention:
but with the well advised is wisdom.
Proverbs 13:10

60.
SIXTY

Be at her side when she needs you. Everything
else can wait. Be sensitive to her needs,
and show her that she is a priority.

In all things approving ourselves as the ministers of God,
in much patience, in afflictions, in necessities, in distresses.
2 Corinthians 6:4

61.

SIXTY-ONE

Take her on weekend getaways as often as you can
afford to. Sometimes life keeps us so busy that we
just need to drop what we are doing and get away
from everything. It will be good for both of you.

This is something we do as often as we can. Sometimes we
don't go very far from home. We just go. It's necessary to keep our
minds and hearts fresh. These are times we usually need to get
refocused or create new directions. It is also good to get away from
all the chores at home and just "do nothing" for a change.

62.
SIXTY-TWO

Exercise with her. I know you both
need it, and if you want to live longer
for each other, you've got to do it.

Exercise! We all need it anyway, the older we get. If you just
go for walks together, or maybe a jog, it is good for both of you to
do it together. Tena and I work out in our garage with exercise
equipment, and we are usually seen around the neighborhood
walking. Exercising together helps encourage one another.

63.

Be a communicator. Call her if you are going to be late or if you are bringing home unexpected company. Spend time talking about life's issues with her. Learn to have good conversation.

Do not forget to do good and to share with others.
Hebrews 13:16 NIV

Many times we go out to eat and are amazed that so many people have nothing to say to each other. How can you have nothing to say to your spouse? Learn to have good conversation with your wife. Talk about dreams, goals, the kids, her work or your work, current events, spiritual matters, or whatever helps keep up with each others' lives.

64.
SIXTY-FOUR

Clean her jewelry for her. Once again, it's those small
things that mean a lot. This helps her save time, too.

Thy cheeks are comely with rows of jewels.
thy neck with chains of gold.
Song of Solomon 1:10

65.
SIXTY-FIVE

Smell good! Why is this so hard to get
across to some men? Get some cologne,
splash it on, and watch her light up.

Ointment and perfume rejoice the heart.
Proverbs 27:9

66.
SIXTY-SIX

Make long-term goals and plans with her.
This shows commitment to her and says that
you plan on being there for a long time.
(It also reinforces your vow, "til, death do us part.")

Sometimes we differ a little on long-term goals. I'm thinking of paying the house off one day. She's thinking about the new house she wants to live in next year. I'm looking forward to when the kids are grown, and she's wanting to adopt a baby girl. It's really fun to plan and scheme life's goals and dreams. The more we talk about our goals and plans, the more we discover we really do have very much in common.

67.
SIXTY-SEVEN

Express yourself, men! It's okay to say "thank you,"

"I'm sorry," or "I love you." Let her know

exactly where you stand and how you feel.

The words of a wise mans mouth are gracious.
Ecclesiastes 10:12

This will help to carve you into her heart. It builds trust, unity,
and continues to strengthen the bond between you.

68.
SIXTY-EIGHT

If you can, surprise her with not just one
new outfit, but *two*. Sacrifice something
for yourself if you have to. She's worth it.

You can do this. Get to know her style, her taste in clothes, and
most of all, her size. I've done this several times, and she is amazed
at how I choose just what she likes—size and everything. It can
really be fun.

69.
SIXTY-NINE

Plan the family vacation. Pick the place, pack the bags, load the car, and get going. You might not even tell her where you are going. Just let it be a surprise.

70.
SEVENTY

Do the ironing sometimes. This will give you a whole new appreciation for the art.

Hint: Ask first about the settings if you are not sure. This may be the first and last time for you to do the ironing.

Whatsoever thy hand findeth to do, do it with thy might.
Ecclesiastes 9:10

71.
SEVENTY-ONE

Buy her a pet if she doesn't have one.
Who can resist a cute puppy or a tiny kitten?

Hint: Stay away from snakes, lizards, or the like.
Believe me, they won't have the same effect.

72.
SEVENTY-TWO

Encourage your wife in every way possible if she is
trying to lose weight. She is already sensitive about
it, so help encourage her. Let her know how good
she looks to you and how proud you are of her.

Hint: Do not eat dessert in front of her at this point.

73.

SEVENTY-THREE

Put on your old clothes and help her do the spring cleaning. (For some people, this may take all spring, but two can finish faster than one.)

Now, this is definitely work, but you can live through it. I promise. It sometimes can take all spring, but we usually find things we had forgotten about and many things we'd like to forget about. Actually, most of our spring cleaning results in a garage sale, and we usually make a little money while we are at it.

74.
SEVENTY-FOUR

Keep the toilet seat down. All the time. 'Nuf said.

Folly is set in great dignity, and the rich sit in low place.
Ecclesiastes 10:6

75.
SEVENTY-FIVE

Gently brush her hair. It's good for her hair,
and she will tell you it feels wonderful. Try it!

76.
SEVENTY-SIX

Send her encouraging thoughts during the day
by e-mail! Whether she works at home or away
from home, encouraging e-mail can help her
get through the day. (Who would have ever
imagined this possible just a few years ago?)

Let your speech be always with grace. seasoned with salt.
Colossians 4:6

I can't imagine what we did before e-mail and cell phones.
Sometimes we get so busy with work and family responsibilities that
the only time we can say hello through the day is bye e-mail. What a
fantastic means of communication! There are so many cool things
you can do through the Internet, including sending her a virtual
bouquet of flowers or other greeting ideas. Use it to your advantage.

77.
SEVENTY-SEVEN

If you live where it gets cold in the winter, keep a fire going inside for her. Nothing warms the atmosphere like a glowing fire on a cold day. Later in the evening, make hot chocolate or coffee and just sit in front of the fire with her. (My wife and I find this is a great time to just think about old times and share our future dreams and goals.)

Godliness with contentment is great gain.
1 Timothy 6:6

78.
SEVENTY-EIGHT

Lie on her side of the bed before
she gets there just to warm it for her.
She will really appreciate this.

I know this sounds silly to some of you, but when it's cold in the house, I guarantee you will benefit from warming the bed for her. If you just can't lie there and warm it, at least get her an electric blanket and turn it on in advance. Either that, or she will put her cold feet all over you. (I hate when that happens.)

79.
SEVENTY-NINE

Climb in the tub or shower with her sometimes

and help wash her hair or wash her back.

This is a great time to just pamper her.

We really do this quite often. I usually get in the shower to wash her back, and, of course, she washes mine. Age doesn't matter here. This is just good, "clean" fun.

80.
EIGHTY

Always try to be a step ahead of her in thinking of things and taking care of things. There always seem to be errands to run, clothes to put away, cars to wash, bills to pay, or any number of little things. Just be a thinker and get them done.

Whatsoever ye do in word or deed, do all in the name of the Lord Jesus.
Colossians 3:17

81.
EIGHTY-ONE

Live up to, and go far beyond, her wildest expectations of what a husband should be. It's a decision, a choice, that you can make.

82.
EIGHTY-TWO

Stop on the way home from a trip or an outing
and pick up some fresh flowers. No special
reason, just a "because I love you" gesture.

The flowers appear on the earth;
the time of the singing of birds is come.
Song of Solomon 2:12

What woman can resist fresh flowers? Don't save up for an
anniversary or special holiday. Do this as often as you can. This
creates a positive and loving environment. Life is so short; we need
to take every opportunity to use every gesture we can to say. "I love
you." Don't take her for granted.

83.
EIGHTY-THREE

If your wife is sick in bed or just not feeling well,
be there by her side to take care of her every need.

Above all these things put on charity, which is the bond of perfectness.
Colossians 3:14

84.
EIGHTY-FOUR

Get up and make the coffee (or tea)
in the morning, and bring her a cup.

*That I may come unto you with joy by the
will of God, and may with you be refreshed.*
Romans 15:32

85.
EIGHTY-FIVE

Talk about your wife to your friends. Brag about the
things she does, and tell them how lucky you are.
This does as much good for you as it does for her.

I thank my God upon every remembrance of you.
Philippians 1:3

I find it easy to talk about my wife because I'm so nuts about
her. She goes far beyond what I ever imagined a wife could be. In
fact, when I tell people about all she does for me out of pure love,
they usually find it too hard to believe. If I could package all she is,
I'd make a fortune, but having Tena makes me a very rich man.

75

86.
EIGHTY-SIX

Write her mother a letter, thanking her for all the
years she poured her own life into your wife.
Thank her for instilling all those fantastic qualities
you love about your wife. (If you have not had a
great relationship with your mother-in-law up to
this point, I'll bet this will help turn things around.)

Let your light so shine before men, that they may see your
good works, and glorify your Father which is in heaven.
Matthew 5:16

87.
EIGHTY-SEVEN

Let your wife have the remote control for the
TV sometimes. Compromise instead of conflict.

I have to admit, I'm not very good at this one. We like the
same type of news-magazine programs, and that's about all we
watch. But, sometimes, when flipping through the channels, we
come across a good ball game or something, and we don't watch it
long enough. So, we now have the picture-in-picture feature on our
TV. This way we can both watch what we want.

88.

Go for walks with your wife—morning or evening, whichever you prefer. This can be part of that exercise routine, and it's a great way to spend time talking about your day. Hold her hand for added benefit.

"If someone forces you to go one mile, go with him two miles."
Matthew 5:41 NIV

Walking is so good anyway, so why not go with your wife? We use this time to talk, catch up, and get our exercise. This is very valuable time that we spend together and should be treated as such. Tena and I are always out walking in the neighborhood, which also gives us the opportunity to say hello to people we do not know. It is a testimony of your marriage as well.

89.
EIGHTY-NINE

Have a picture of yourself framed and sent to her while she is away on business or other travel. You could send it with a "missing you" letter or card. She is probably a little lonely for home and family anyway, and this will give her a little bit of "home" while she is away. It will bring a smile to her face and a glow in her heart.

Blessed are they that mourn: for they shall be comforted.
Matthew 5:4

90.
NINETY

Massage her feet when she is dead tired. Whether she's been at work, out shopping, looking after the home, or caring for children, she'll really appreciate this.

91.

Don't complain about things! It doesn't do
any good, it's not godly, and neither of you
need to hear it. I promise it won't help
the mood around your household.

Do all things without murmurings and disputings.
Philippians 2:14

Now, we all do this now and again. But for your sake and hers,
try to keep it to a minimum. Complaining about anything does no
good. It is not a good example to your children (if you have any),
and it's only going to irritate your wife. You don't like to hear her
complain, so don't be a part of it either.

92.
NINETY-TWO

Keep her checkbook balanced for her. It's not
that she can't do it, but you might have to
suggest that she S-L-O-W down the spending.

Thou wilt keep him in perfect peace, whose mind is stayed on thee.
Isaiah 26:3

This is a safeguard for me, if nothing else. Tena writes checks
the way kids eat candy—often. It's not that she can't balance it
herself. It's just that she doesn't take the time to do it, so she's
usually unaware that there may be danger ahead.

93.
NINETY-THREE

Read to her. (My wife loves this.)
Just curl up together somewhere and
read something that uplifts and touches her.

Blessed is he that readeth, and they that hear the words.
Revelation 1:3

Tena loves to lie in bed at night and have me read to her. I usually read an inspiring story, whether it's from the Bible or an article I came across in a magazine or newspaper. We love to read stories of people who have overcome great odds trying to accomplish something. Try reading something uplifting to your wife. It's great for your spirits.

94.
NINETY-FOUR

Always let your wife know how much you appreciate
the little things she does for you: cleaning up a
mess, straightening your tie, putting away your
clothes, or just bringing you a cup of coffee.
(The little things make a house a home
and should certainly be appreciated.)

This is where so many men fail. We forget to say "thank you"
for all the things she takes the time to do for us. This should go
both ways. We should do the simple little things for her as well.
We should be doing everything we can to promote harmony and
peace. Create the environment you want by being appreciative
and reciprocating.

95.

NINETY-FIVE

If she wants to make a career change,

be the first to support the idea and

help her find another career.

*Seek ye first the kingdom of God . . . and
all these things shall be added unto you.*
Matthew 6:33

96.
NINETY-SIX

Earn her complete trust in everything you do.

Boy, this is a big one! This boils down to being faithful. Not just in terms of other women, but in everything you do and say. You will prove your loyalty and devotion to her throughout life. Be a man to be counted on. Be faithful to her wherever you go. Prove to be trustworthy. She should know she can count on you.

97.
NINETY-SEVEN

Be the spiritual leader in your home in all things.

Be an example of giving, serving,

leading others, and praying.

Thou shalt love the Lord thy God with all thy heart, and with
all thy soul, and with all thy mind, and with all thy strength.
Mark 12:30

98.

When traveling together, carry her luggage.
(Oh man, this can be tough. I sometimes
need a crane to lift it. But hey, I usually
get my exercise taken care of)

My yoke is easy, and my burden is light.
Matthew 11:30

I cant tell you how many times I've traveled and seen a woman carrying more luggage than her husband. How ignorant can this guy be? It disgusts me how some men treat their wives. If you cannot carry her bags when traveling because you have too many, then pay someone to help out. Don't be seen as an uncaring man who expects his wife to lift heavy things.

99.
NINETY-NINE

Spoil her with as many signals of love as you can.
A ribbon around the tree when she arrives home,
love notes tucked here and there, gifts, surprises,
flowers, music, voice mail. There should never
be any doubt about your love for her.

There is no magic formula I can offer you for spoiling your wife. You know her—what she likes, what she doesn't like. You know what she expects, and what would make her happy. Every woman is different. Do what you know your wife would love. We are creating memories every day of our lives, so make sure your memories are ones you want to leave behind.

*Blessed is the man that walketh not in the counsel
of the ungodly, nor standeth in the way of sinners,
nor sitteth in the seat of the scornful.*

*His delight is in the law of the Lord; and in his law doth
he meditate day and night. And he shall be like a tree planted by
the rivers of water, that bringeth forth his fruit in his season; his
leaf also shall not wither; and whatsoever he doeth shall prosper.*

Psalm 1:1-3

100.
ONE HUNDRED

Plant a tree in honor of your wife.

Watch as it takes root, grows, and becomes a beautiful example of what she means to you: strong, with many branches, a place that provides shade, a place for the birds to nest, and a tree whose roots grow deep to support the outward beauty and protection it offers. Over the years you will need to love, nurture and protect your tree so that it may grow to be all it was intended to be. But with the right care, your tree will bring you joy for years to come. And your wife will be honored by it.

101.
ONE HUNDRED ONE

Last, but not least (in fact most important),
be a godly man. Everything you do in your life
should reflect the Lord God who made you both.
This will be your testimony to God and to all
who observe your life. I know that if you live a
life pleasing to God, you will certainly be a pleasing
husband to her. Seek ways to serve others
in your life, but let it start at home.

Honour all men. Love the brotherhood. Fear God.
1 Peter 2:17

The most valuable suggestion I can offer you is to read your Bible. The best way to become the man God wants you to be is to find out more about Him. Learn about God. Get to know what He likes and what He expects you to be. Understand what God says your role as a husband is and live it. Seek His face, and spend time in prayer.

A NOTE FROM THE AUTHOR

So often it is we men who fail in our marriages. Sometimes we bring on needless pain or sorrow by our actions. We are to be the leaders in our home. To be an effective leader, we must seek the answers we need from God and live in accordance with the way He wants us to live.

The most beautiful thing God gave us on earth is our wives. He knew exactly what man needed when he created woman. He knew how our wives would love us, excite us, fill our desires, and be our companions. He knew everything you and I needed and wanted in a wife. I thank God every day for supplying me with just what I needed in a wife and friend. I could not make it without her. I rely on her for strength and wisdom when mine have failed. I count on her love to keep me going. I need her support through the challenging times and her comfort when I have nowhere else to go.

You may read this book and be inspired to spoil your wife as never before. You may come up with 101 ideas of your own. Spoiling your wife should be done on an unconditional basis. No strings attached. I believe that whatever circumstance you are in now, you can begin seeing your wife in a whole new light. Start treating her the way she deserves, and watch how it changes and enhances your relationship.

God bless you, my friend!

SPECIAL THANKS:

I would like to thank my father, Walter Brown, for giving me a perfect example of how to love my wife. Dad is a godly example of what we are commissioned to do as husbands. He showed me by his example how to love, give, sacrifice, lead, train, walk faithfully, pray, cry, and just spoil my wife.

My mom (Kathy) and dad still spoil each other. They go for walks and hold hands, pray together, dream together, laugh together, and cry together.

Thanks to both of you for giving your three children good role models in marriage, teaching each of us our place and responsibility. I am convinced that our country is in the trouble it is in today because of the lack of commitment to making our homes a wonderful place.

Thank you, Mom and Dad, for holding the light and for sharing with us the greatest gift: Jesus!

ABOUT THE AUTHOR

Ron Brown has been married to Tena since 1992. She describes him as "sweet, creative, unique, and multi-talented" and says he spoils her on a regular basis. "Every woman dreams of having the perfect man," she says, "and Ron is the perfect man for me."

Ron is the father of two teenage sons, who authored the book *101 Ways Kids Can Spoil Their Parents*, and he frequently helps his public-speaking wife write speeches. He is a sales and marketing professional who has an intense interest in landscape design and exterior beauty. His entrepreneurial spirit led him to start his own company in 1996, which he recently sold. He is now the director of marketing for a large site planning and landscape development company.

According to his wife, Ron has "an amazing creative flair for everything"—from antiques and collectibles to cars and art. He studied marketing and real estate in college. Ron sings and plays the trumpet and frequently shares his musical gift at churches and in weddings.

The Browns make their home in Arlington, Texas.

If you would like to contact the author, you may write to him at this e-mail address: 101ways@home.com